Contents

Welcome	2
1 My toys	8
2 My family	18
3 Move your body	28
4 My face	38
5 Animals	48
6 Food	58
7 Clothes	68
8 Weather	78
Goodbye	88
Festivals	92
Extra practice	96
Picture dictionary	104

Welcome

1 ✏️ Match. Then write.

Hello.
I'm Rose.

_____.
I'm Uncle Dan.

Hello.
_____ Charlie.

Hello. I'm
_____.

Lesson 1

  **Find and colour. Then write.**

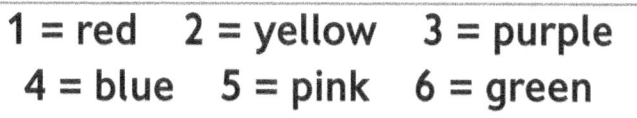

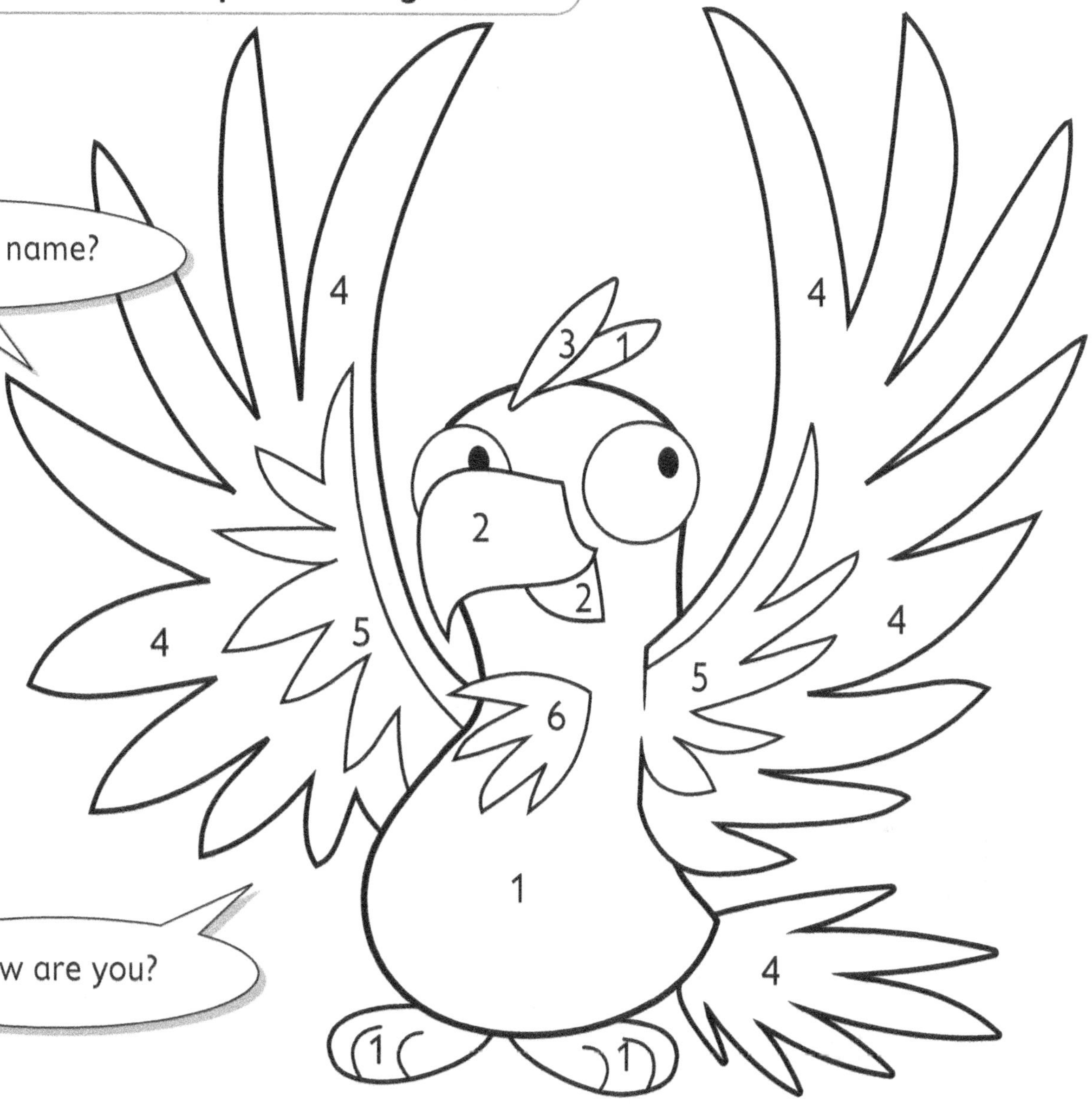

What's your name?

How are you?

I'm _____. And how _____?

My name's _____.

Lesson 2

3  **Find and write.**

yaMdon _Monday_   Fayrid _____

daTsuey _____   taSrayud _____

deWsenyad _____   dunSay _____

hurTdyas _____

4 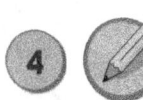 **Complete. Then read and say.**

Monday

Tuesday

Wednesday

Thursday

Friday

Hop up and down

Stamp your feet

Say Hurray!

Jump up and down

Clap your hands

Lesson 3

5 Write and circle. (~~dogs~~ parrots   rabbits   snakes)

6 Read and write.

Yes, I do.   No, I don't.

1 Do you like parrots?   _____

2 Do you like fruit?   _____

3 Do you like vegetables?   _____

4 Do you like Mondays?   _____

Lesson 4

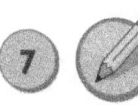 **7** Find and circle the words.

E	N	M	J	U	N	E	D	L
B	O	A	P	R	I	L	E	J
A	V	Y	L	G	E	O	C	A
U	E	J	U	L	Y	C	E	N
G	M	A	R	C	H	T	M	U
U	B	C	S	J	I	O	B	A
S	E	P	T	E	M	B	E	R
T	R	H	P	B	D	E	R	Y
F	E	B	R	U	A	R	Y	A

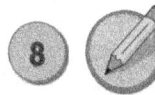 **8** Follow and write.

1. My birthday is in __October__. I'm _____.

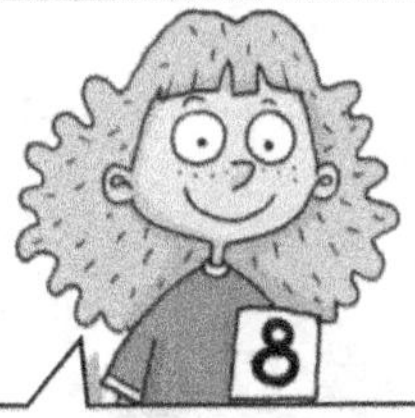

2. My birthday is in _____. I'm _____.

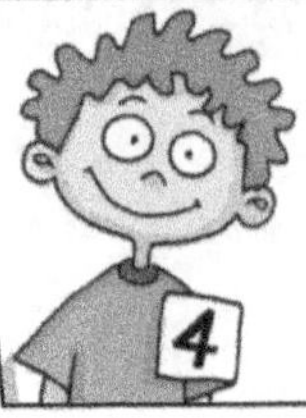

3. My birthday is in _____. I'm _____.

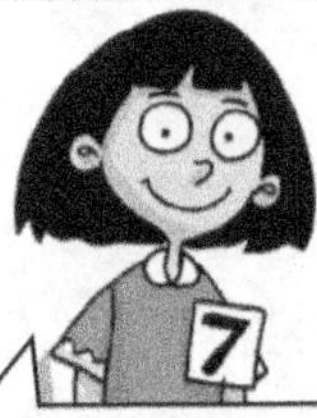

a. July

b. October

c. January

6 Lesson 5

9 Read and match. Then listen and check.

1 What's your name?
2 How old are you?
3 When's your birthday?
4 What's your favourite colour?
5 Do you like dogs?
6 What day is it today?
7 How are you?

a It's in August.
b I'm fine, thank you!
c My name's Rose.
d Blue.
e It's Tuesday.
f I'm eight.
g Yes, I do.

10 Ask a friend and answer.

1 What's your name?

2 What day is it today?

3 How are you today?

Lesson 6

1 My toys

1. Follow and write.

~~ball~~ bike boat car doll kite lorry teddy bear train

Lesson 1

2   Look. Then read and circle.

1 ((What's) / What are) this?

It's a (ball / (doll) / teddy bear).

2 (What's / What are) that?

It's a (boat / bike / train).

3 (What's / What are) these?

They're (kite / kites / lorries).

4 (What's / What are) those?

They're (bikes / bike / ball).

3   Listen and write. Then draw and colour.

1  2  3

It's a _train_. They're _____. It's a _____.

It's _____. They're _____. It's _____.

_____.

Lesson 2

9

 **Look and count. Then write.**

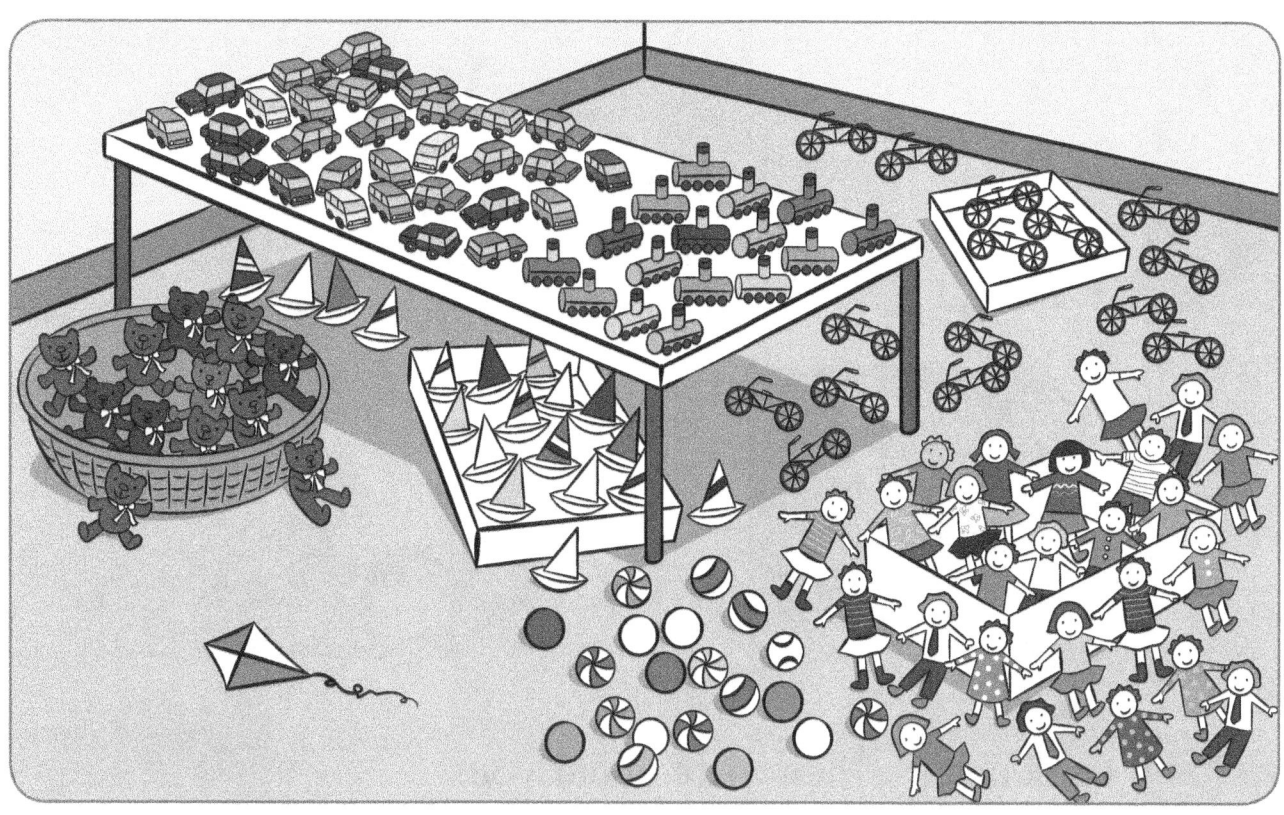

① How many _____bikes_____ are there?
There are ___fifteen bikes___.

② _____ are there?
There are _____.

③ _____ are there?
There are _____.

④ _____ are there?
There is _____.

   **Look and number. Then tell the story again.**

1

  **Look and ✓. Then write about you.**

1   2

Good friends play together and share toys.

Good friends listen and help.

Think of a good friend.

_____ is a good friend.

What do you like?

We like _____

and _____.

12 Lesson 5

9  Read the words and circle.

~~fish~~   rich   shell   ship

10  Listen and link the letters.

START — ch — c — h — sh
        p   f   b   FINISH
   s   sh   ch   s

11  Listen and write the words.

1 ch i n   2 ___ ___ ___

3 ___ ___ ___   4 ___ ___ ___

12 Read aloud. Then listen and check.

I can see a fish. I can see a shell.

Lesson 6

13     Look and write. Then find and draw the missing word.

bike   boat   bus   car   ~~helicopter~~   lorry   plane   train

1. ¹H E L I C O P T E R
2. 
3. 
4.  
5. 
6. 
7. 
8.

14 Look through your window. Count and write.

cars ☐   bikes ☐   buses ☐   motorbikes ☐
lorries ☐   trains ☐   planes ☐   helicopters ☐

Lesson 7

15 Complete the picture and match.

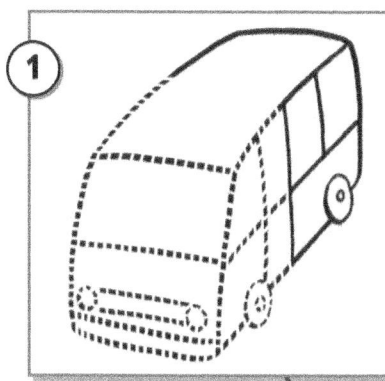
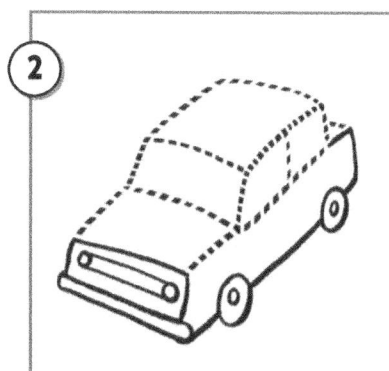
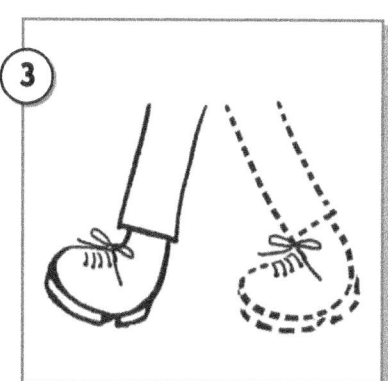

a I walk to school.
b I go to school by bus.
c I go to school by car.

16 Read and write. How do you travel?

by bike   by boat   by bus   by car
by helicopter   by lorry   by plane   by train

1 I go to the library _____.
2 I go to the shop _____.
3 I go to the park _____.
4 I go to school _____.

Lesson 8

17  Read and circle. Then colour.

 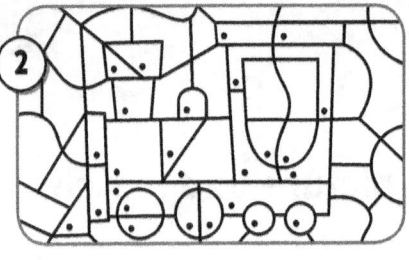 

It's a ((car) / boat). It's a (bike / train). It's a (doll / teddy bear).
It's blue. It's yellow. It's purple.

18  Look and circle. Then write.

(What's this?) / What are those?   What's this? / What are these?

It's a ___*boat*___ .   They're _____ .

What's that? / What are these?   What's that? / What are those?

_____   _____

19 Look at Activity 18. Count and write.

1 How many cars are there? There are _____ cars.

2 How many balls are there? _____

Lesson 9

20  Read and write. Then colour.

bike ~~favourite~~ school teddy bear

These are my
¹ _favourite_ toys.
This is my favourite
² _____ bear. His
name's Fred and he's brown.

And this is my ³ _____.
It's red and black. I go to
⁴ _____ by bike.

21 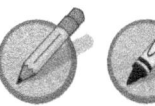 Draw your favourite toys. Then write.

These are my favourite toys.
_____
_____
_____
_____
_____

Lesson 10

2 My family

1  Look and write.

> aunt ~~cousin~~ daughter
> grandad granny son uncle

This is my dad.

This is my mum.

This is my brother.

1 This is my _cousin_.

2 This is my _____.

3 This is my _____.

4 This is my _____.

5 This is my _____.

6 This is my _____.

7 This is my _____.

18 Lesson 1

2  Look, circle and write.

~~aunt~~   cousin   daughter   son

1 Who's (he / (she))?

(He's / (She's)) my ___aunt___.

2 Who's (he / she)?

(He's / She's) my _____.

3 Who's (he / she)?

(He's / She's) my _____.

4 (He's / She's) my _____.

Lesson 2

 Look, read and write.

~~attic~~   bedroom   flat   hall   kitchen   living room

Where's my granny?

She's in the ___attic___.

Where's my uncle?

He's in the _____.

Where's my aunt?

_____ in the _____.

Where's my daughter?

_____ in the _____.

Where's my son?

_____ in the _____.

Where's my cousin?

_____ in the _____.

  **Read and colour.**

1 The red car is on the bed.
2 The purple car is behind the backpack.
3 The blue car is under the chair.
4 The yellow car is on the desk. It's next to the lamp.
5 The green car is in the backpack.

 **Look at the picture again. Write *True* or *False*.**

1 There are two beds.   _____True_____
2 There are three desks.   _____
3 There are six cars.   _____
4 There's a lamp on the desk. _____

Lesson 4

6     Read and circle. Then match.

1   Where's Charlie's grandad?
    He's in the (flat / (shop)).

2   Where's Charlie's mum?
    She's in the (garden / bathroom).

3   Where's Charlie's uncle?
    He's in the (shop / kitchen).

4   Where's Charlie's aunt?
    She's in the (attic / library).

7 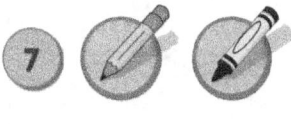   Read and write.
    Then draw your family.

How many aunts have you got?
_I've got_____.

How many uncles have you got?
_____

How many cousins have you got?
_____

 **Read the words and circle.**

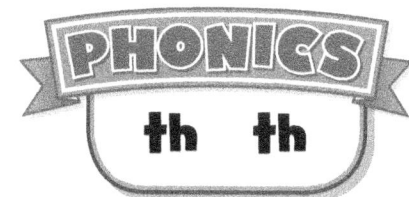

~~bath~~   thick   thin   this

9 🎧 **Listen and link the letters.**

```
         s           th          th          sh
START        a           r           s              FINISH
         th          z           ch          th
```

10 🎧 **Listen and write the words.**

1 th i s   2 _____

3 _____   4 _____

11   **Read aloud. Then listen and check.**

This is a thick book. That is a thin book.

Lesson 6

 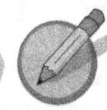 Listen and number. Then write.

baby   children   grandparents   ~~parents~~

a

_____

b

_____

c  1

parents

d

_____

13  Read and match.

They're young.   She's young.   They're old.   He's young.

Lesson 7

Wider World

14 Look and write.   garden   house   treehouse

1. This is a _____.
2. This is a _____.
3. This is a _____.

15 A treehouse home! Listen and number.

Lesson 8

 **Read and write. Then match.**

1 Where's my daughter?
   _____She's_____ in the garden.

2 Where's your aunt?
   _____ in the house.

3 _____ my cousin?
   He's in the flat.

  **Read and draw.**

My teddy bear is in the bathroom.

My ball is on the bed.

My kite is next to the ball.

My doll is under the bed.

18 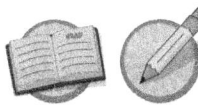 Read and write.

~~aunt~~   garden   one   these   two

This is my uncle and
¹ _aunt_ and
² _____ are my cousins.

They are in my ³ _____.

I've got ⁴ _____ cousins. They are babies.

They're ⁵ _____ year old.

19  Draw some of your family. Then write.

This is my _____
and _____.
_____
_____
_____
_____

3 Move your body

1 Look and write.

> clap   move   nod   point   ~~shake~~   stamp   touch   wave

<u>Shake</u> your body.   _____ your arms.   _____ your head.

_____ your toes.   _____ your feet.

_____ your fingers.   _____ your hands.   _____ your legs.

  **Read and circle.**

①

(He / (She)) can shake
(his / (her)) body.

②

I (can / can't) touch
(my / your) toes.

③

(He / She) can stamp
(his / her) feet.

④

I (can / can't) wave
(my / your) arms.

   **Listen and number.**

a

b

c

d

Lesson 2

 **Look and match. Then write the missing letters.**

1.    ____ ____ the splits

2.   c ____ tch a b ____ ll

3.   clim ____

4.    thr ____ ____ a b ____ ll

5.   stand on your h ____ ____ d

6.    swi _n_ _g_

7.    do cartwh ____ ____ ls

8.   swi ____

Lesson 3

5 Look, write and circle.

climb   do cartwheels   ~~do the splits~~   swim

1 Can he *do the splits*?

Yes, he can. / No, he can't.

2 Can you _____?

Yes, I can. / No, I can't.

3 Can he _____?

Yes, he can. / No, he can't.

4 Can you _____?

Yes, I can. / No, I can't.

  **Read and match.**

1. "Jump! Touch your toes!"
2. "This is fun!"
3. "Er, can you help? It's the bus."
4. "You can push fast!"

 a
 b
 c
 d

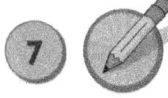 Write ✓ = exercise or ✗ = not exercise.

 1 ✓
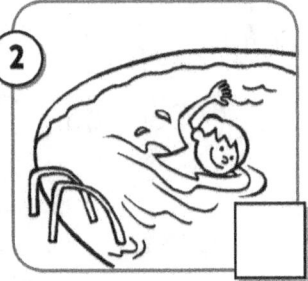 2
 3
 4

 5
 6
 7
 8

8  Read the words and circle.

ink ~~ring~~ sing sink

9 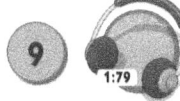 Listen and link the letters.

START — g — nk — ng — c

n — sh — th — FINISH

ng — k — m — nk

10  Listen and write the words.

1 p i ng   2 ___ ___ ___
3 ___ ___ ___ 4 ___ ___ ___

11   Read aloud. Then listen and check.

Dad can sing. The girl can sing.

Lesson 6

12  **Look and write.**

~~hop~~
pull
push
skip

13   **Read and find. Then number.**

☐ Wave your arms.
☐ Jump.
☐ Clap your hands.
☐ Touch your toes.
☐ Skip.
1 Hop.

Lesson 7

Wider World

14 Look and match.

 1
 2
 3
 4

a) tug of war   b) sack race   c) egg-and-spoon race   d) three-legged race

15 Read and write about yourself.

| Yes, I can.   No, I can't. |

1 Can you run fast? _____
2 Can you kick a ball? _____
3 Can you touch your toes? _____
4 Can you point your toes? _____
5 Can you throw a ball? _____

Lesson 8

16 Look and write.

| climb | do the splits | hop | skip | swim | swing |

1. Can she __climb__?
Yes, she can.

2. Can he _____?
_____, he can't.

3. Can he _____?
Yes, _____.

4. Can _____?
_____.

5. _____?
_____.

6. _____?
_____.

17 What can you do? Read and circle.

1 I (can / can't) do cartwheels.
2 I (can / can't) swim.
3 I (can / can't) stand on my head.
4 I (can / can't) hop.
5 I (can / can't) do the splits.
6 I (can / can't) run fast.
7 I (can / can't) catch a ball.
8 I (can / can't) climb trees.

Lesson 9

18 Look and read. Then write *can* or *can't*.

I ¹ _can_ shake my body and I ² _____ skip. I ³ _____ catch a ball and I ⁴ _____ do cartwheels. I ⁵ _____ hop. And I ⁶ _____ touch my toes!

19 Look and ✓ or ✗. Then write about yourself or a friend.

I can _____
and I _____.
_____
_____
_____
_____

Lesson 10   37

4 My face

1 Look and write.

ears   eyes   ~~face~~   hair   mouth   nose

1. face
2. ___
3. ___
4. ___
5. ___
6. ___

Lesson 1

2 Read. Then look and write *1* or *2*.

a) I've got big eyes. `2`
b) I've got short hair. ☐
c) I haven't got a big mouth. ☐
d) I've got long hair. ☐
e) I've got small eyes. ☐
f) I haven't got a big nose. ☐

3 Look, read and circle.

1 Have you got small ears?

(Yes, I have.) / No, I haven't.

2 Have you got long hair?
Yes, I have. / (No, I haven't.)

3 Has she got big eyes?
Yes, she has. / No, she hasn't.

4 Has he got a small nose?
Yes, he has. / No, he hasn't.

Lesson 2

  **Read and circle.**

1
She's got
((long) / short)
hair.

2
She's got
(neat / messy)
hair.

3
He's got
(long / short)
hair.

4
She's got
(neat / messy)
hair.

5
He's got
(blond / dark)
hair.

6
He's got
(straight / curly)
hair.

  **Listen and ✓. Then draw.**

- ✓ big eyes
- ☐ big nose
- ☐ short, curly hair
- ☐ small eyes
- ☐ small nose
- ☐ long, straight hair

Lesson 3

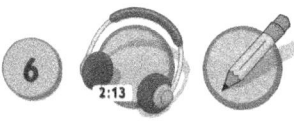

Listen and circle. Then look and write.

1 (straight) / curly / (messy) / blond   It's ___Ruth___.
2 messy / neat / blond / red   It's _____.
3 long / short / straight / curly   It's _____.
4 messy / neat / curly / dark   It's _____.

7 Look at Activity 6 and write.

1 Granny has got ___short, curly hair_____.
   Her hair is ___short and curly_____.

2 Ruth has got _____, _____ hair.
   Her hair is _____ and _____.

3 Max has got _____, _____ hair.
   His hair is _____ and _____.

4 Uncle Ed has got _____, _____ hair.
   His hair is _____ and _____.

5 I've got _____, _____ hair.
   My hair is _____ and _____.

Lesson 4

8  **Look and write.**

1 Has she got a ___small___ nose?
   Yes, she _____.
2 _____ got black hair.
   He _____ got blond hair.
3 Her _____ is long.
4 _____ hair is messy.

| hair |
| has |
| hasn't |
| He's |
| His |
| ~~small~~ |

9  **Listen and number.**

a

b

c    1

d

Lesson 5

10 Read the words and circle.

~~snail~~ rain tail feet

11 Listen and link the letters.

START — a — ee ai e a o
         u   ai ee FINISH
                 i   ai

12 Listen and write the words.

1 s ee

2 _____

3 _____

4 _____

13 Read aloud. Then listen and check.

The cat has got a tail. The cat has got four feet.

Lesson 6

14  **Count and write.**

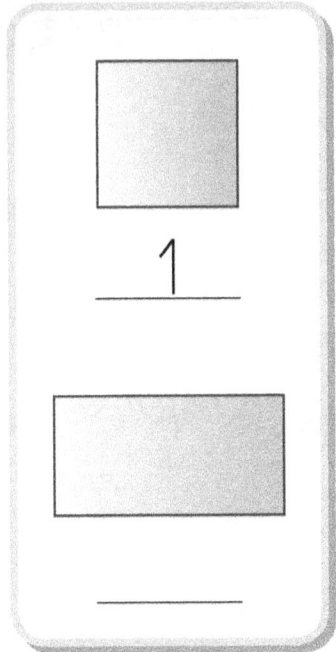

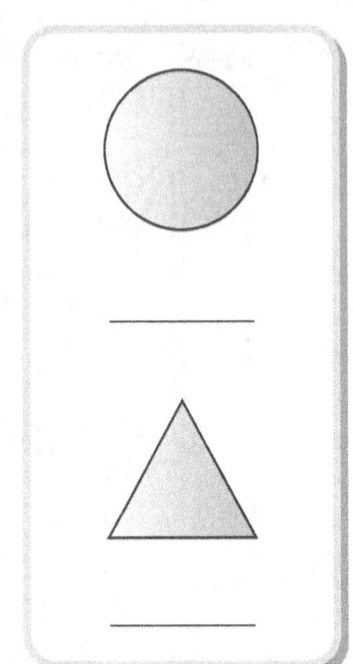

15  **Listen, look at Activity 14 and circle.**

1 (Yes) / No   2 Yes / No   3 Yes / No   4 Yes / No

16  **Draw. Use the shapes in Activity 14. Then write.**

It's a _____.

Wider World

17  Read and circle.

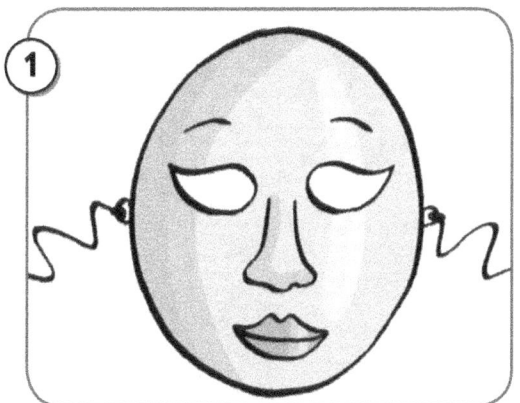

1. It's a (painting / (mask)).
It's got (big / small) eyes.

2. It's a (mosaic / statue).
It's got (long / short) hair.

18   Look at the mosaic pictures. Colour and write.

What's this?

It's a _____.

What's this?

_____

Lesson 8

  **Read and write.**

1 Has she got big eyes?
   Yes, she has.

2 Has she got dark hair?
   _____.

3 Has she got small ears?
   _____.

4 Has she got a big nose?
   _____.

  **Draw. Then read and write.**

1 He's got short, blond hair. It's curly. Who is it? It's ___Nick___.

2 She's got long, blond hair. It's straight and messy.
  Who is it? _____

3 She's got long, blond hair. It's curly and neat.
  Who is it? _____

 **Read and circle.**

This is me and my best friend. ¹((His) / Her) name's George.

My hair is short and ²(dark / blond). I've got ³(big / small) eyes. My eyes are brown. I've got a ⁴(big / small) mouth and ⁵(big / small) ears!

George's hair is ⁶(long / short) and ⁷(dark / blond). His hair is ⁸(neat / messy). He's got ⁹(big / small) eyes and a ¹⁰(big / small) mouth.

   **Draw yourself and a friend and write.**

me

This is me and my best friend.

Lesson 10

5 Animals

1 Look and write.

cow   duck   ~~goat~~   hen   horse   sheep   turkey

1. goat
2. ___
3. ___
4. ___
5. ___
6. ___
7. ___

2 Listen and number.

a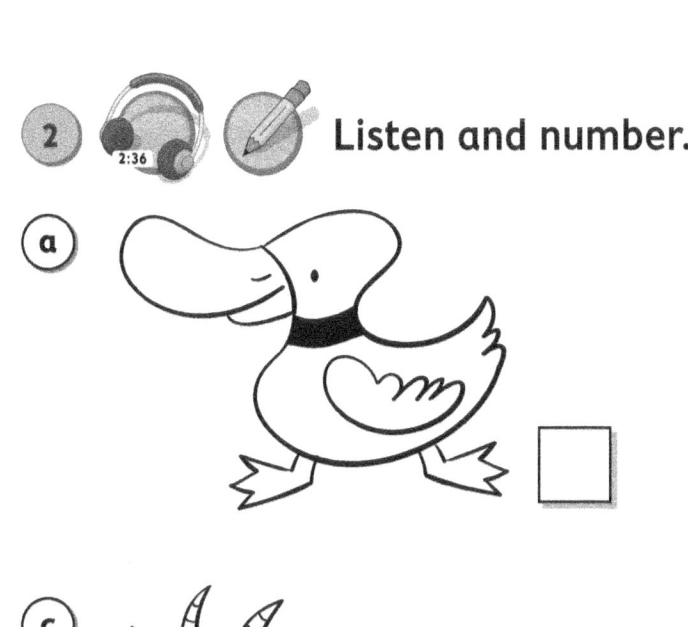

b

c

d  `1`

3 Look at Activity 2. Read, write and colour.

1 What are these? They've got big bodies and black feet. They're white. They've got black faces. They're ___sheep___.

2 What's this? It's got a big mouth and two big feet. It's yellow. It's a _____.

3 What's this? It's got four legs. It's brown. It's a _____.

4 What are these? They're big and black. They've got long legs. They're _____.

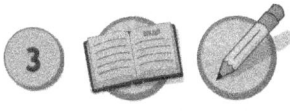

4 Look and write.

~~bat~~ crow fox frog lizard owl rat skunk

1. bat
2. _____
3. _____
4. _____
5. _____
6. _____
7. _____
8. _____

5 Read, match and write.

1 It's got a long tail.
   It's brown.

   a   They're _____.

2 They're small and green.
   They've got big eyes.

   b   It's a _fox_.

3 They're thin and black.
   They've got two legs.

   c    They're _____.

50 Lesson 3

6 **Read and circle the mistakes. Then write.**

1

It's a frog. It's (big).
It isn't _big_. It's _small_.

2

They're goats. They're very thin.
They aren't _____.
They're _____.

3

It's a duck. It's big.
It isn't a _____.
It's a _____.

4

They're skunks. They're green.
They aren't _____.
They're _____ and _____.

7 **Look at Activity 6 and write the answers.**

Yes, it is.   ~~No, it isn't.~~   Yes, they are.   No, they aren't.

1 Is the hen small?   _No, it isn't._
2 Are the foxes thin?   _____
3 Is the frog small?   _____
4 Are the skunks red?   _____

Lesson 4

8 Read and draw.

What's that?

1 It's a cow.
2 It's a goat.
3 They're hens.
4 It's a skunk.

9 Look and match.

1 — c
2 — 
3 — 
4 —

a 
b 
c 
d

52 Lesson 5

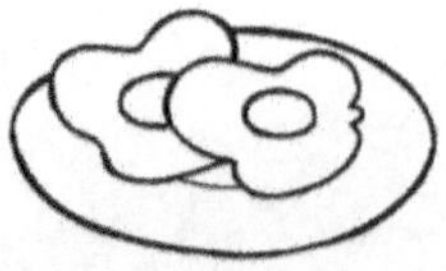

10  Read the words and circle.

~~boat~~ goat light soap

11 Listen and link the letters.

START — i — oa ... ch ... i ... igh ... FINISH

(a, igh, o, a, oa, igh)

12 Listen and write the words.

1 s igh   2 ___ ___
3 ___ ___   4 ___ ___ ___

13   Read aloud. Then listen and check.

The goat has got some soap. The goat has got a boat.

Lesson 6

14  Look and read. Then write and circle.

1  I'm a ___fox___.
I'm (asleep / awake) in the day.

2  I'm a _____.
I'm (asleep / awake) at night.

3  I'm an _____.
I'm (asleep / awake) at night.

4  I'm a _____.
I'm (asleep / awake) in the day.

5  I'm a _____.
I'm (asleep / awake) in the day.

| bat |
| cow |
| duck |
| ~~fox~~ |
| owl |

15  Draw the animals from Activity 14.

day

night

54 Lesson 7

Wider World

5

16 Look and match.

 1 a hen

 2 an ostrich

 a — a chick

 b — an egg

 c — a chick

 d — an egg

17 Read and write *True* or *False*.

1 Ostriches are birds. ____True____
2 They aren't big. They're small. _____
3 They've got two legs. _____
4 They've got very short legs. _____
5 They can't fly. _____
6 The father ostrich is brown. _____
7 Ostrich eggs aren't small. They're big. _____

18 Correct the false sentences.

Ostriches are big.
_____

Lesson 8

55

19  Listen, ✓ and colour.

1 a 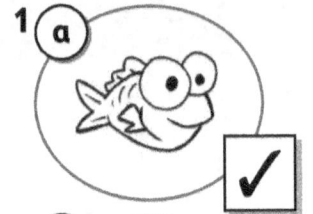 b    2 a  b

3 a  b    4 a  b

20  Look, read and write.

1 Is the cow big?
   Yes, it is.

2 Are the sheep white?
   _____

3 Is it a hen?
   _____
   It's an _____.

4 Are they foxes?
   _____
   They're _____.

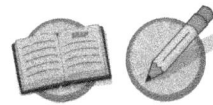 **Read and write.**

asleep awake big fox four horse tail ~~white~~

My favourite animal is very big and
¹ _white_ .

It's got ² _____ legs and a long ³ _____ .

It's got a ⁴ _____ nose.

It's ⁵ _____ in the day.

It's ⁶ _____ at night.

Is it a ⁷ _____ ?

No, it isn't. It's a ⁸ _____ !

 **Draw your favourite animal. Then circle and write.**

My favourite animal is (big / small) and _____ .

It's got _____

_____

_____

_____

_____

Lesson 10

6 Food

1 ✏️🖍️ **Look and write. Then draw.**

1	*eggs*	🍳	✓
2	_____	🥗	✗
3	_____	🍕	✗
4	_____	🍗	✗
5	_____	🐟	✓
6	_____	🍚	✓
7	_____	🍎	✓
8	_____	🍌	✗
9	_____	🍔	✗

apples
bananas
burgers
chicken
~~eggs~~
fish
pizza
rice
salad

58 Lesson 1

2  **Look and write.**

apples   bananas   ~~chicken~~   eggs

I like _chicken_.

I don't like _____.

She likes _____.

He doesn't like _____.

3 **Look at Activity 2. Read and match.**

1 Does Charlie like apples?
2 Does Rose like chicken?
3 Does Ola like bananas?
4 Does Uncle Dan like eggs?

a) Yes, she does.
b) No, he doesn't.
c) Yes, she does.
d) No, he doesn't.

4 **Read and answer.**

1 Do you like burgers? _____
2 Do you like salad?   _____

Lesson 2

5 Look and match.

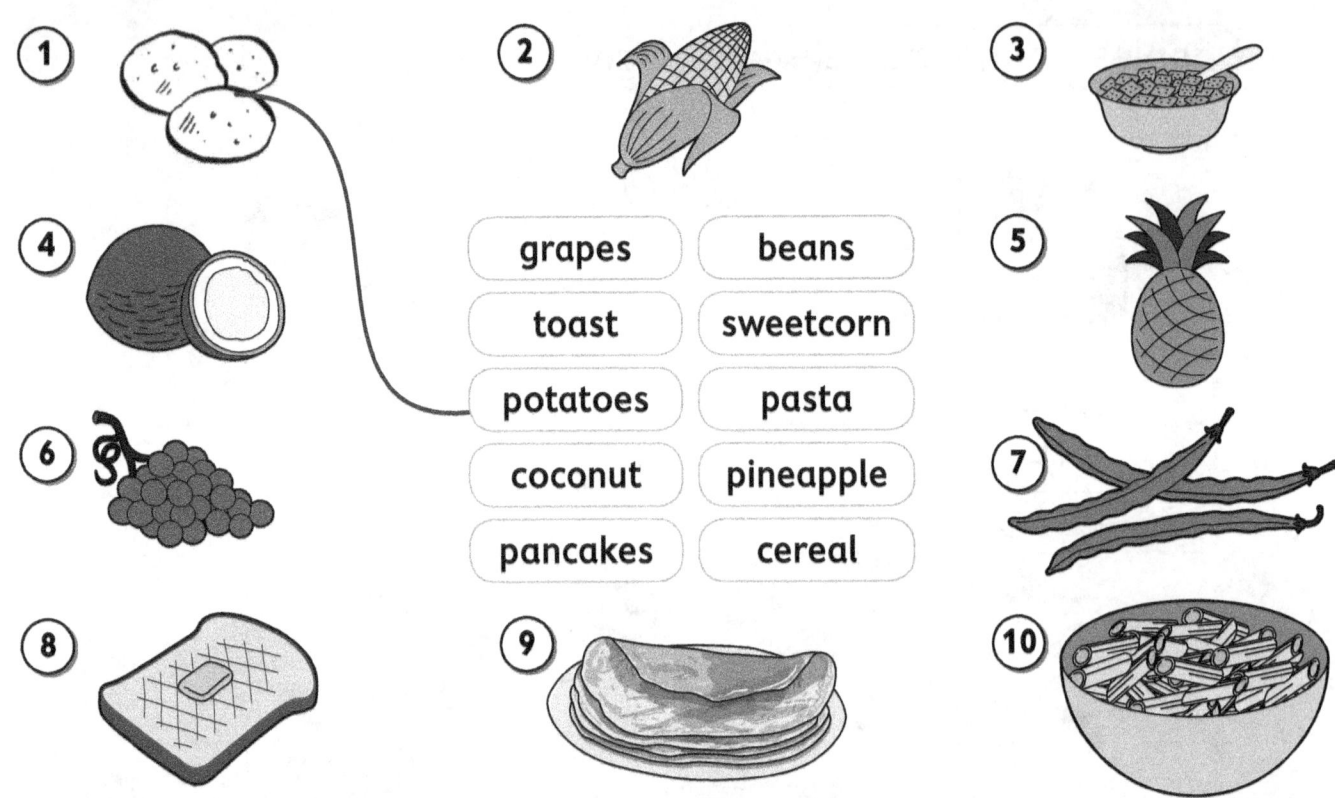

grapes · beans · toast · sweetcorn · potatoes · pasta · coconut · pineapple · pancakes · cereal

6 Look and write. Then read and number.

~~breakfast~~ dinner lunch

1. breakfast
2. _____
3. _____

a. I like chicken and apples.
b. I like toast and eggs. **1**
c. I like fish and vegetables. I don't like rice.

60 Lesson 3

7 Look and write.

cereal

grapes

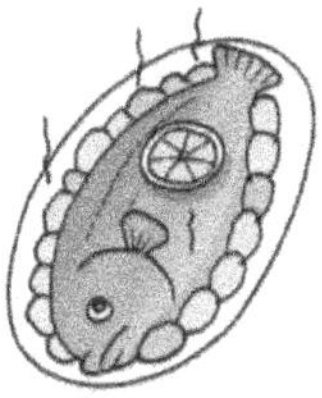

fish

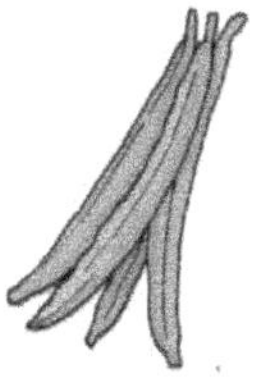

beans

There's some...

rice
_____
_____
_____

There are some...
_____
_____
_____
_____

burgers

rice

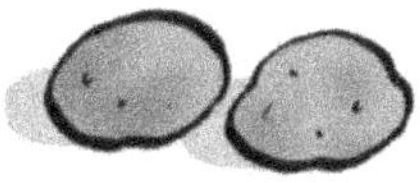

potatoes

chicken

8 Look at Activity 7. Read and write the answers.

~~Yes, there is.~~   No, there isn't.   Yes, there are.   No, there aren't.

1 Is there any rice?   _Yes, there is._
2 Is there any pizza?   _____
3 Are there any bananas?   _____
4 Are there any burgers?   _____

Lesson 4

9 Read and ✓.

	YES	NO
1 Charlie likes apple juice.	✓	
2 Rose doesn't like apples.		
3 Uncle Dan likes pineapple for lunch.		
4 Ola likes banana milkshakes.		
5 Charlie's favourite cake is chocolate cake.		
6 Uncle Dan likes chicken and rice for dinner.		
7 Rose likes milk.		
8 Charlie likes salad for dinner.		

10 Look and circle the healthy food and snacks.

1  2 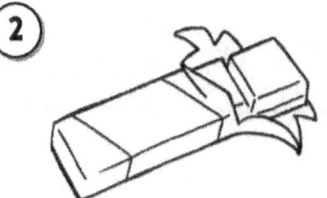 3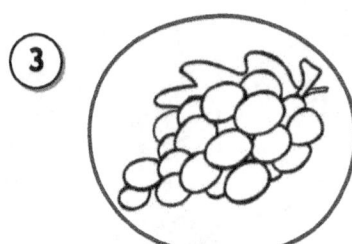

4  5  6

7 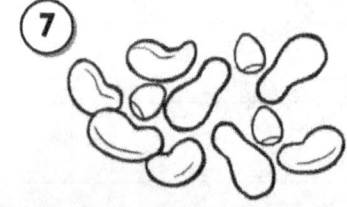 8  9

11  Read the words and circle.

~~book~~   foot   look   moon

12 Listen and link the letters.

START — oo — a

ee   igh   e   oa
        oo   o   FINISH
   ai   ai   oo

13 Listen and write the words.

1 t oo

2 ___ ___

3 ___ ___ ___

4 ___ ___ ___

14   Read aloud. Then listen and check.

Look at the big moon. Look at the book, too.

Lesson 6

15 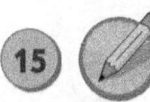 Look and write. cook ~~cut~~ fry mix

1. cut   2. _____   3. _____   4. _____

16  Recipes. Read and write.

1  Hot fruit salad

a
___Cut___ some fruit.

b
_____ the fruit in a pan.

c
_____ the _____.

2 Pasta salad

a
_____ some pasta.

b
_____ some sweetcorn.

c
Mix the _____ and _____.

3 Fish and chips

a
_____ some _____.

b
_____ some potatoes.

c
_____ the potatoes.

64 Lesson 7

Wider World

17  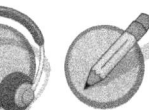 **Listen and circle.**

1 She likes ( /  / )

   for ((breakfast) / lunch / dinner).

2 He likes ( /  / )

   for (breakfast / lunch / dinner).

3 He likes ( /  / 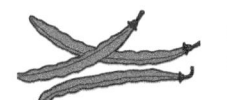)

   for (breakfast / lunch / dinner).

18   **Complete the sentences and write about food in your country.**

	me	my friend
Do you like mushrooms for breakfast?		
Do you like pasta for lunch?		
Do you like fish and chips for dinner?		
Do you like _____ ?		
Do you like _____ ?		
Do you like _____ ?		

Lesson 8

19   **Listen and circle. Then write.**

I like…
cereal
chicken
cheese
fish
apples
salad

I don't like…
toast
pizza
bread
bananas
eggs
rice

1 He _likes chicken_ and _____.

2 He _____ or _____.

 20 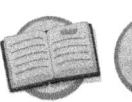 **Read and circle. Then draw.**

This is my breakfast.
There's ((some)/ any) cereal and there's (some / any) toast.
There are (some / any) bananas and there's (some / any) juice.
There isn't (some / any) cheese and there aren't (some / any) apples.
I like breakfast!

21  Read and write.

any like don't fruit ~~some~~

This is my favourite dinner.
There's ¹ _some_ pizza and there's some salad.
I ² _____ pizza and salad.
There aren't ³ _____ burgers. I ⁴ _____ like burgers.
And there's some fruit. I like ⁵ _____.
But I don't like bananas.

22   Draw your favourite dinner and write.

This is my favourite dinner.
_____
_____
_____
_____
_____
_____

Lesson 10

7 Clothes

1 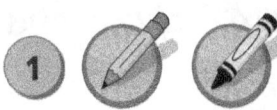 Find and write. Then colour.

dress   hat   jacket   skirt   shoe   socks   ~~T-shirt~~   trousers

1 an orange T-shirt   2 blue _____
3 a pink _____   4 a red _____
5 a brown _____   6 green _____
7 a purple _____   8 a black _____

Lesson 1

2 Read and colour. Then read and write.

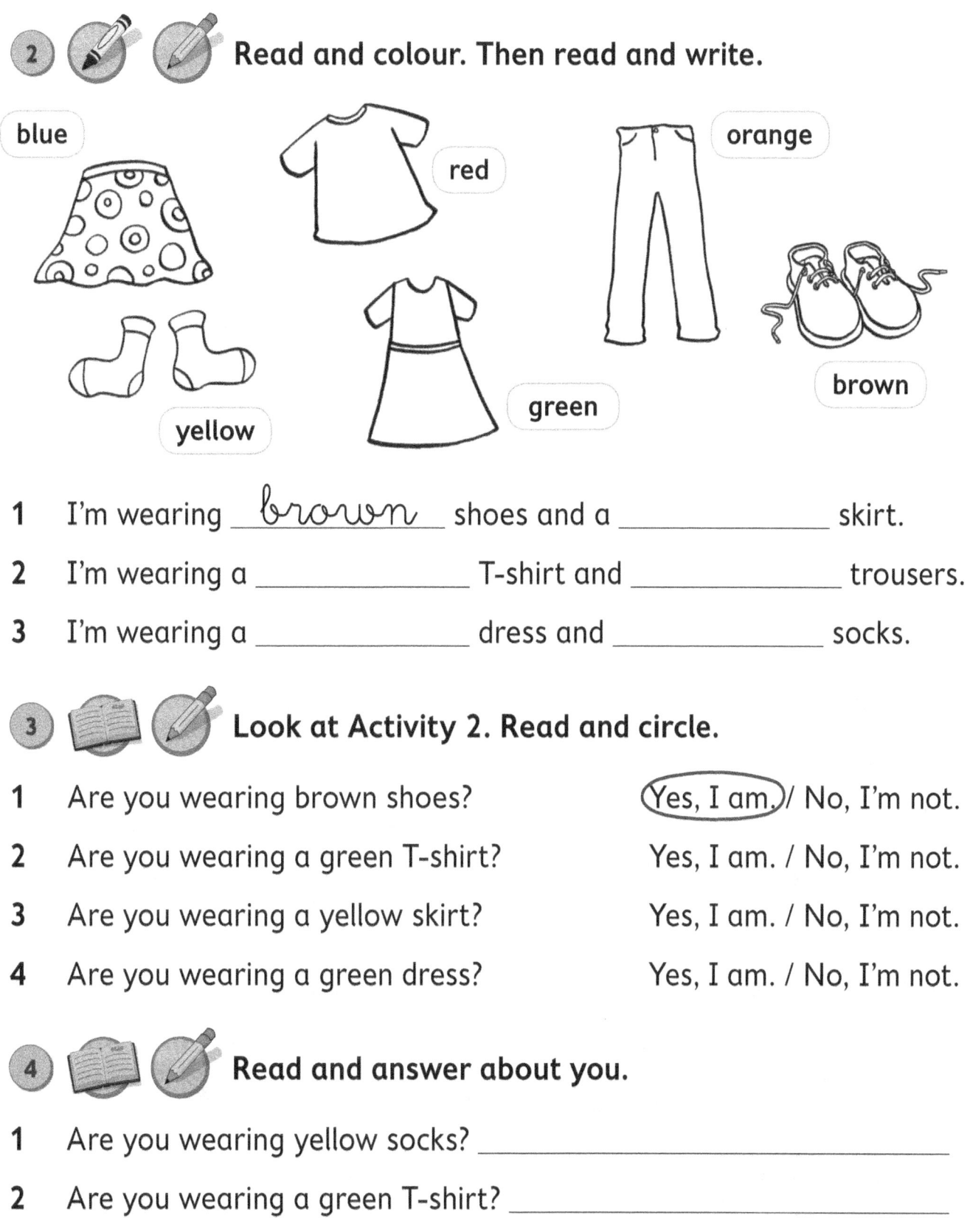

1 I'm wearing ___brown___ shoes and a _____ skirt.

2 I'm wearing a _____ T-shirt and _____ trousers.

3 I'm wearing a _____ dress and _____ socks.

3 Look at Activity 2. Read and circle.

1 Are you wearing brown shoes?   (Yes, I am.)/ No, I'm not.

2 Are you wearing a green T-shirt?   Yes, I am. / No, I'm not.

3 Are you wearing a yellow skirt?   Yes, I am. / No, I'm not.

4 Are you wearing a green dress?   Yes, I am. / No, I'm not.

4 Read and answer about you.

1 Are you wearing yellow socks? _____

2 Are you wearing a green T-shirt? _____

3 I'm wearing _____.

4 I'm not wearing _____.

Lesson 2

5  Look and write.

bed   boots   jumper   ~~pyjamas~~   pyjamas   school   shoes   T-shirt

1
Take off your *pyjamas*.

2
Put on your _____.

3
Put on your _____.

4
It's time for _____.

5
Take off your _____.

6
Take off your _____.

7
Put on your _____.

8
It's time for _____.

Listen and match. Then colour.

Look, read and circle. Then colour.

Would you like a red jumper?
(Yes, I would) / No, I wouldn't.
I'd like a (red jumper / red shirt).

Would you like white trainers?
Yes, I would. / No, I wouldn't.
I'd like (a pink boot / pink boots).

Would you like a yellow jacket?
Yes, I would. / No, I wouldn't.
I'd like a (yellow shirt / yellow skirt).

Would you like blue pyjamas?
Yes, I would. / No, I wouldn't.
I'd like (a blue pyjamas / blue pyjamas).

8   Colour. Then write.

1 I'm wearing a _____ _____.

2 I'm wearing a _____ _____.

9   Look and write.

~~Good morning.~~   Goodbye!   Good night.
I'm sorry.   Please.   Thank you.

Good morning.

PHONICS 7

ar   ir
or   ur

10 Read the words and circle.

~~car~~   girl   shark   surf

11 Listen and link the letters.

START — ir — or   ur   r
         o   ck   ir   FINISH
         ar   ai   ch   ar

12 Listen and write the words.

1 s ir   2 __ __

3 __ __   4 __ __

13 Read aloud. Then listen and check.

See the girl surf. See the shark surf!

Lesson 6

14  Look and write.

chef   firefighter   ~~nurse~~   police officer

1. She's a *nurse*.
2. He's a _____.
3. He's a _____.
4. She's a _____.

15 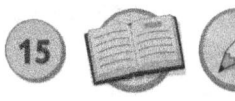 Read. Then look at Activity 14 and number.

a. I'm wearing a shirt, a black skirt and black shoes. I'm wearing a hat. ☐

b. I'm wearing a white dress, a hat and black shoes. I'm not wearing a helmet. 1

c. I'm wearing a coat and boots. I'm wearing a big helmet. ☐

d. I'm wearing a T-shirt and trousers. I'm wearing white shoes and a tall hat. ☐

Wider World

7

16   Colour and play.

a    b

Are you wearing a yellow shirt?

Yes, I am.

No, I'm not.

17  Look at Activity 16 and write.

I'm wearing a _____ shirt and a _____ skirt. I'm wearing _____ boots. And I've got a _____ hat with flowers on it!

I'm wearing _____ trousers and a _____ jacket. I'm wearing _____ shoes. And I've got a _____ hat!

Lesson 8

18 Listen and ✓.

1	purple dress ☐	pink dress ✓	pink skirt ☐
2	black trainers ☐	white trainers ☐	blue shoes ☐
3	purple skirt ☐	purple dress ☐	pink skirt ☐
4	brown shoes ☐	red socks ☐	red shoes ☐

I CAN DO IT!

19 Read and number. Then colour.

1 I'm wearing yellow pyjamas.
2 I'm wearing red shoes.
3 I'm wearing black boots.
4 I'm wearing a purple jumper.

a ☐   b ☐   c 1   d ☐

20 What are you wearing? Read and circle.

1 Are you wearing pink pyjamas?   Yes, I am. / No, I'm not.
2 Are you wearing white socks?   Yes, I am. / No, I'm not.
3 Are you wearing black shoes?   Yes, I am. / No, I'm not.
4 Are you wearing glasses?   Yes, I am. / No, I'm not.

Lesson 9

21 Read and write. Then colour.

are   is   like   these   this   ~~wearing~~

I'm ¹ _wearing_ my favourite clothes. ² _____ are my favourite jeans and ³ _____ is my favourite T-shirt. My jeans ⁴ _____ blue and my T-shirt ⁵ _____ red. I'm not wearing black trainers. I'm wearing white trainers. I'd ⁶ _____ some black trainers. I'm wearing a green cap.

22 Draw your favourite clothes and write.

I'm wearing my favourite clothes.

_____

_____

_____

_____

_____

Lesson 10

77

8 Weather

1  Look and write.

cloudy   rainy   snowy   stormy   ~~sunny~~   windy

It's __sunny__.   It's _____.   It's _____.

It's _____.   It's _____.   It's _____.

Lesson 1

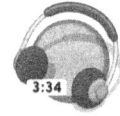  **Listen and write. Then draw.**

rainy   ~~snowy~~   sunny   windy

1 He likes _snowy_ days.

2 She doesn't like _____ days.

3 She likes _____ days.

4 He doesn't like _____ days.

   **Read, write and circle.**

1 What's the weather like today?   It's _____.

2 Do you like sunny days?   Yes, I do. / No, I don't.

3 Do you like cloudy days?   Yes, I do. / No, I don't.

4 Do you like stormy days?   Yes, I do. / No, I don't.

Lesson 2

4  Look and write.   ride   take   fly   go   ~~make~~   read

Let's _make_ a snowman.

Let's _____ for a walk.

Let's _____ a bike.

Let's _____ a photo.

Let's _____ a kite.

Let's _____ a book.

5   Look, read and write.

Monday	Tuesday	Wednesday	Thursday	Friday	Saturday
windy	sunny	cloudy	rainy	stormy	snowy

1 It's snowy. What day is it today?   It's _Saturday_.

2 It's windy. What day is it today?   It's _____.

3 It's rainy. What day is it today?   It's _____.

4 It's sunny. What day is it today?   It's _____.

5 It's stormy. What day is it today?   It's _____.

6 It's cloudy. What day is it today?   It's _____.

80   Lesson 3

 **Look and circle.**

 **Follow and write *his* or *hers*.**

a. These shoes are ___hers___.

b. These trainers are _____.

c. This kite is _____.

d. This bike is _____.

8  Look and number. Then write.

It's _____ .

It's ____*rainy*_____ .

It's _____ .

It's _____ .

9  Look and ✓ the things you can share with other people.

	friend(s)	sister(s)	brother(s)	parents

10  Read the words and circle.

~~boy~~   cow   cowboy   down

11  Listen and link the letters.

ar   o   h   w

START   j   oy   oy   FINISH

ow ——— y   p   ow

12  Listen and write the words.

1 owl   2 _____

3 _____   4 _____

13  Read aloud. Then listen and check.

The boy watches the cowboy. The cow watches the boy.

Lesson 6

14   Look and write. Then listen and number.

~~cold~~   freezing   hot   warm

1
cold

15  Read, look and ✓ or ✗.

Monday	Tuesday	Wednesday	Thursday	Friday	Saturday	Sunday
☀	🌬	🌧	🌨	☀	⛈	☁

1 It's Tuesday. It's windy. ✓   2 It's Saturday. It's stormy. ☐

3 It's Thursday. It's rainy. ☐   4 It's Sunday. It's cloudy. ☐

5 It's Monday. It's snowy. ☐   6 It's Friday. It's sunny. ☐

16 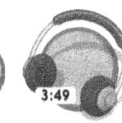  **Listen and write.**

| ~~August~~ January July March September |

1. It's _August_.
It's _summer_. It's sunny.

2. It's _____.
It's _____. It's windy.

3. It's _____.
_____
_____ snowy.

4. _____
_____
_____

17  **What's your favourite weather? Read and write.**

My birthday is in _____.
The weather is _____.
My favourite month is _____.
The weather is _____.

Lesson 8

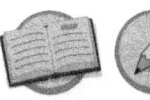 Read, look and write *A* or *B*.

Picture A

Picture B

1 It's cloudy. **A**
2 I'm wearing a T-shirt and trousers.
3 I've got a train.
4 I like pizza.
5 I'm wearing a dress.
6 I've got a doll.
7 I like chicken.
8 Look at my dog. It's big.
9 It's sunny.
10 I'm wearing boots.

19  **Read and write.**

> boots   cold   ~~December~~   doesn't   hat   snowman

My favourite month is
¹ December.
It's ² _____ and snowy in my country. I'm wearing a coat and big ³ _____.
This ⁴ _____ is mine. He's got a ⁵ _____!
My cat ⁶ _____ like the snow.

20  **Draw your favourite month and write.**

My favourite month is
_____.
_____
_____
_____
_____
_____

Lesson 10   87

Goodbye

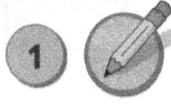 **1** Look and write.

> ~~castle~~ cave clothes dinner doctor
> farmer mountain shopping

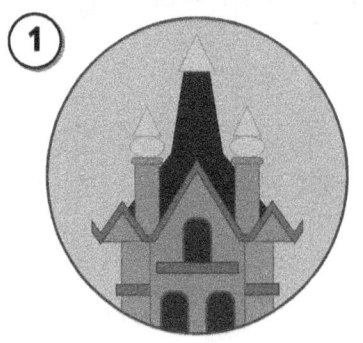  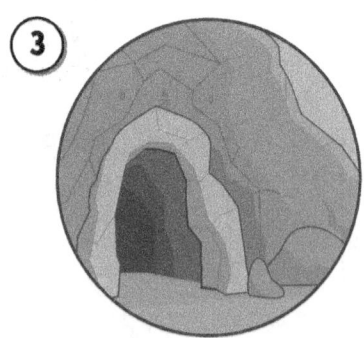

castle _____ _____

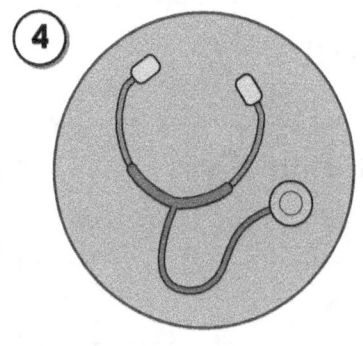  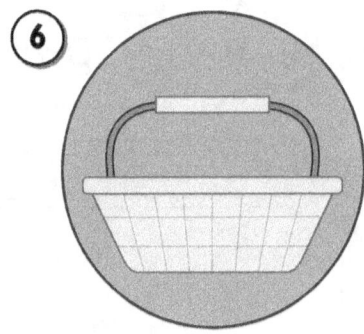

_____ _____ _____

_____ _____

Lesson 1

 Read and draw.

1   There's a photo on the TV.
2   There is a key in the door.
3   There are some shoes under the sofa.
4   There's a duck in the box.
5   There are some sunglasses next to the lamp.
6   There's an umbrella behind the bag.

 Look at Activity 2. Read, circle and write.

1   Where (is /(are)) the shoes?   It's /(They're) _under the sofa_.
2   Where (is / are) the duck?   It's / They're _____.
3   Where (is / are) the sunglasses? It's / They're _____.
4   Where (is / are) the photo?   It's / They're _____.

Lesson 2

4  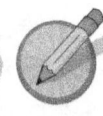 Listen and ✓ or ✗. Then write.

Sally					
has got	✗	✓			
would like	✗				

Sally has got a ___bike___ and an _____.

She hasn't got a _____, a _____ or a _____.

She'd like a _____ and a _____. She wouldn't like a _____.

5  Complete for yourself. Then write.

I've got					
I'd like					

I've got _____.

I haven't got _____.

I'd like _____.

I wouldn't like _____.

6  Can you remember? Read and answer.

1 What colour is Grandad's hair? *It's grey.*
2 Has Rose got curly hair? _____
3 How many cousins has Charlie got? _____
4 Is Charlie wearing a green T-shirt? _____
5 Has Ola got a big nose? _____
6 Is Uncle Dan a doctor? _____
7 Does Charlie like pizza? _____
8 Can Charlie do cartwheels? _____

a) Yes, he does.
b) ~~It's grey.~~
c) No, he isn't.
d) No, she hasn't.
e) No, he can't.
f) Two.
g) No, she hasn't. Her hair is straight.
h) No, it's blue and white.

7 Write three questions for your friend to answer.

1 _____ ? _____
2 _____ ? _____
3 _____ ? _____

Lesson 4

Halloween

1 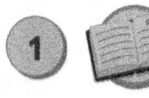  **Read and match.**

1. I'm a witch. I've got six sweets.
2. I'm a monster. I've got a pumpkin.
3. I'm a ghost. I've got four sweets.
4. I'm a pumpkin. I've got a bat.

a
b
c
d
e
f
g
h

2   **Read and circle.**

1. Do you like sweets?   Yes, I do. / No, I don't.
2. Do you like bats?   Yes, I do. / No, I don't.
3. Do you like pumpkins?   Yes, I do. / No, I don't.
4. Do you like Halloween? Yes, I do. / No, I don't.

Christmas

1 ✏️ Look and write.

> card   Christmas tree   present
> sack   ~~Santa~~   star   stocking

① __Santa__   ② _____   ③ _____   ④ _____

⑤ _____   ⑥ _____   ⑦ _____

2 ✏️ Look and colour.

1 = red   2 = green
3 = black   4 = blue
5 = yellow

Christmas

1 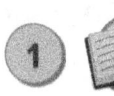 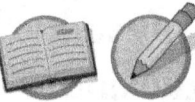 **Read and match.**

1. Wake up, Easter Bunny!
2. Jump, Easter Bunny!
3. Turn around, Easter Bunny!
4. Fall down, Easter Bunny!

a
b
c
d

2 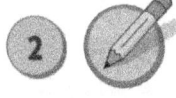 **Count and write.**

1. How many chicks? `5`
2. How many flowers? ☐
3. How many eggs? ☐
4. How many rabbits? ☐

Easter

Summer fun

1 Look and write.

bucket   sand   sandcastle   sea   shell   ~~spade~~

1. spade
2. _____
3. _____
4. _____
5. _____
6. _____

2 Sand art! Join the dots and write.

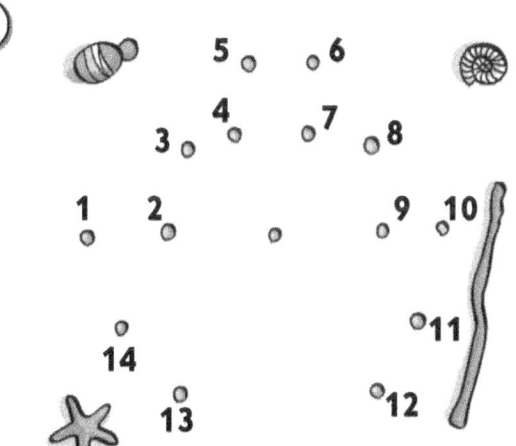

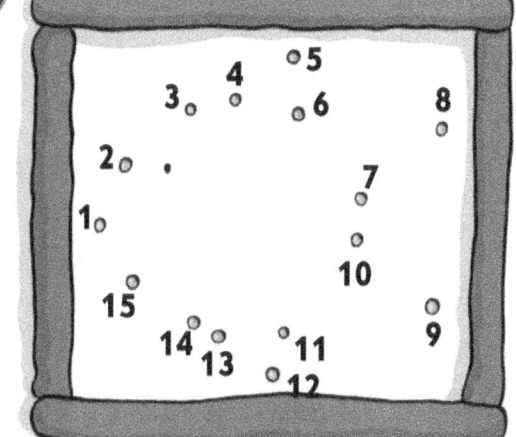

It's a _____.

It's a _____.

Summer fun

1 Write the questions. Then say.

1. name? / your / What's — *What's your name?*
2. are / How / you? _____
3. your / birthday? / When's _____
4. today? / day / What / it / is _____

2 Read and circle. Then write.

1. What's (**this** / that)?
   (**It's** / They're) a _teddy bear_.

2. What are (these / those)?
   (It's / They're) _____.

3. What's (this / that)?
   (It's / They're) a _____.

4. What are (these / those)?
   (It's / They're) _____.

How many cars are there? There are _____ cars.

How many boats are there? _____

96 Unit 1 Extra practice

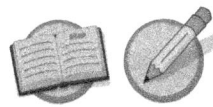 **Read and circle.**

 Who's ((he) / she)?   ((He's) / She's) my uncle.

 Who are (they / there)?   (They're / There) my cousins.

 Where's my aunt?   (He's / She's) (on / under) the sofa.

 **Read and circle.**

1   They're in the (living room / kitchen).

2   (There's / (There are)) two cousins.

3   The doll is (behind / on) the TV.

4   My uncle is next to my (aunt / cousin).

Unit 2 Extra practice

3

1 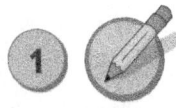 **Choose and write.**

> can   can't   point   touch   ~~wave~~   you

1. ____Wave____ your arms.

2. _____ your fingers.

3. _____ your toes.

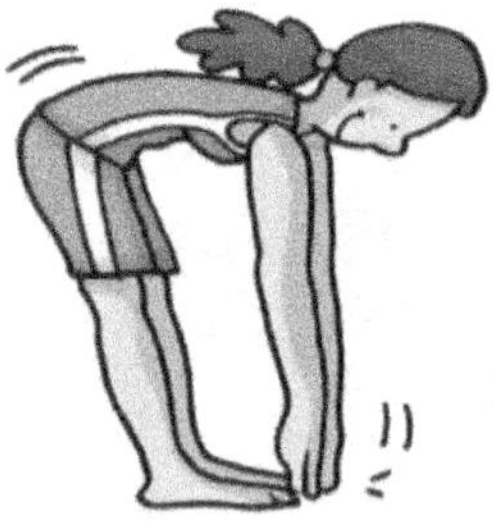

4. Oh, no! I _____ touch my toes.

5. Can _____ touch your toes?

6. Yes, I _____.

1   **Read and draw.**

I haven't got small eyes. I've got big eyes.

I've got a small nose and a small mouth.

I've got big ears. My hair is long and curly.

2 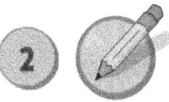 **Write Yes, she has. or No, she hasn't.**

1 Has she got short hair?   *No, she hasn't.*

2 Has she got curly hair?   _____

3 Has she got small eyes?   _____

4 Has she got a small mouth?   _____

3 **Write correct sentences.**

1 She's got a big nose. *She hasn't got a big nose. She's got a small nose.*

2 She's got straight hair. _____

3 She's got small ears. _____

Unit 4 Extra practice

5

1 Circle and write.

It isn't (big /(small)). It's (big / small).

(It's / They're) black.

It's got _____ legs.

(It's / They're) a _____.

(It's / They're) small.

They aren't (black / white).

They're (black / white).

They've got _____ legs.

(It's / They're) _____.

2 Look at Activity 1. Read and match.

1) Are the ducks brown?

2) Is the horse big?

3) Are the ducks small?

4) Is the horse grey?

a) Yes, it is.

b) No, it isn't.

c) No, they aren't.

d) Yes, they are.

1   Read, look and circle.

	🐟	🍕	🍗	🍎	🍌	🍳
👦	✓	✓	✗	✓	✗	✗
👧	✗	✓	✓	✗	✓	✓

1 He ((likes) / doesn't like) fish.

2 She (likes / doesn't like) apples.

3 Does he like bananas? (Yes, he does. / No, he doesn't.)

4 Does she like chicken? (Yes, she does. / No, she doesn't.)

2   Read and circle.

1 There's ((some) / any) cheese.   2 There are (some / any) apples.

3 There isn't (some / any) milk.   4 There aren't (some / any) bananas.

3   Look at Activity 2. Read and match.

1) Is there any cheese?   a) No, there aren't.

2) Is there any pizza?   b) Yes, there is.

3) Are there any apples?   c) Yes, there are.

4) Are there any beans?   d) No, there isn't.

Unit 6 Extra practice

1 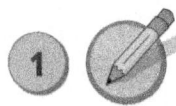 **Choose and write.**

> am are I'm like not purple
> ~~wearing~~ would

1. Are you __wearing__ shoes and socks?

2. Yes, I _____.

3. _____ wearing blue shoes and pink socks.

4. _____ you wearing purple shoes?

5. No, I'm _____.

6. Would you _____ some purple shoes?

7. Yes, I _____. Thank you!

8. Now I'm wearing _____ shoes and pink socks!

102 Unit 7 Extra practice

1 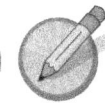 **Choose and write.**

> do   like   mine   that   they're   those
> ~~weather~~   windy

1. What's the ___weather___ like? 
2. It's _____. Good!
3. Do you _____ windy days? 
4. Yes, I _____.
5. What are _____? 
6. _____ kites. 
7. This kite is _____ and _____ kite is yours.
8. I like windy days!

Unit 8 Extra practice

Picture dictionary

Unit 1

Toys

train   bike   ball   car   doll   boat   teddy bear   kite   lorry

 Numbers

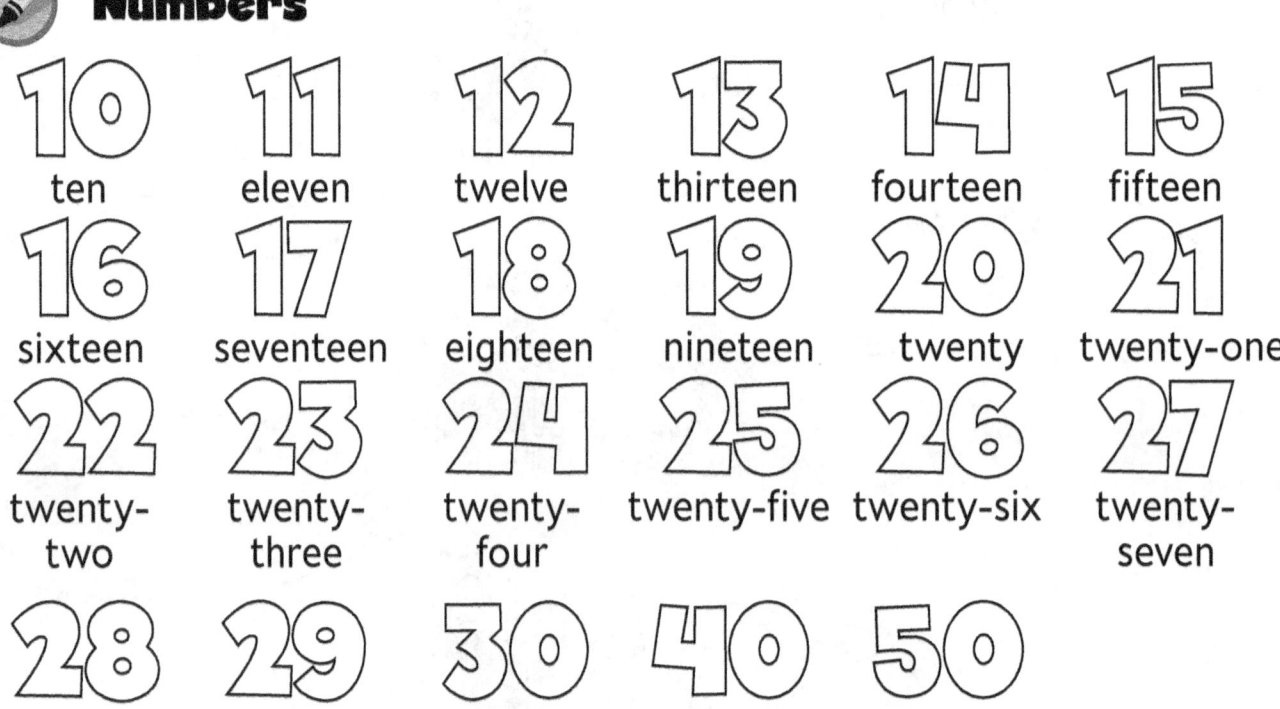

10 ten   11 eleven   12 twelve   13 thirteen   14 fourteen   15 fifteen
16 sixteen   17 seventeen   18 eighteen   19 nineteen   20 twenty   21 twenty-one
22 twenty-two   23 twenty-three   24 twenty-four   25 twenty-five   26 twenty-six   27 twenty-seven
28 twenty-eight   29 twenty-nine   30 thirty   40 forty   50 fifty

Social Science

bus   motorbike   lorry   plane   helicopter

Unit 2

My family

daughter　son　aunt　uncle　granny　grandad　cousins

At home

   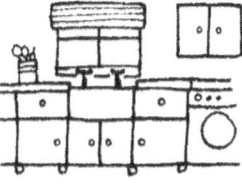

house　flat　hall　kitchen

living room　bedroom　bathroom　attic

Social Science

baby　children　parents　grandparents

young　　　　　　　　　　　　old

Unit 3
Body movements

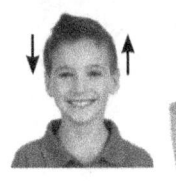

shake your body | nod your head | wave your arms | point your fingers | touch your toes | clap your hands | stamp your feet | move your legs

Actions

swim | climb | catch a ball | stand on your head

throw a ball | swing | do cartwheels | do the splits

 P.E.

pull | push | hop | skip

Unit 4
My face

   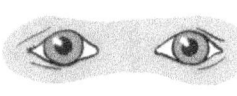 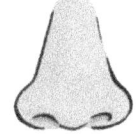 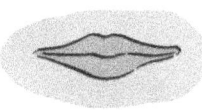

hair   ears   eyes   nose   mouth

 Adjectives

long   short   curly   straight

dark   blond   neat   messy

Maths

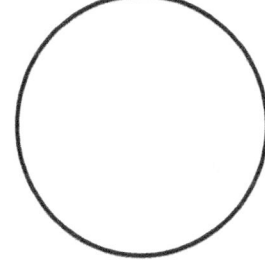 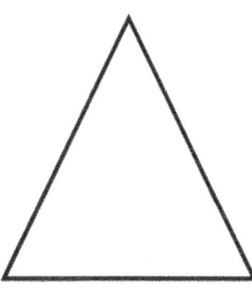  

circle   triangle   square   rectangle

Unit 5
Farm animals

horse — duck — hen — sheep — cow — goat — turkey

 Wild animals

bat — crow — frog — skunk

owl — lizard — rat — fox

 Natural Science

awake — asleep — night — day

Unit 6
Food (1)

  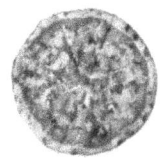  

rice　　　bananas　　　pizza　　　burger　　　fish

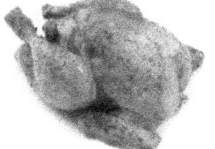   

chicken　　　apples　　　salad　　　eggs

 Food (2)

cereal　　　grapes　　　potatoes　　　pancakes　　　beans

pineapple　　　coconut　　　pasta　　　sweetcorn　　　toast

 Natural Science

 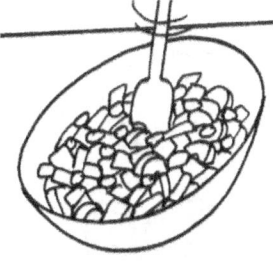  

cut　　　mix　　　fry　　　cook

Picture dictionary

Unit 7
Clothes (1)

 dress
 T-shirt
 socks
 skirt

 shoes
 trousers
 jacket
 hat

Clothes (2)

 pyjamas
 trainers
 shirt
 coat
 jeans

 helmet
 cap
 jumper
 glasses
 boots

Social Science

 nurse
 police officer
 firefighter
 chef

Unit 8

Weather

windy — rainy — sunny — snowy — cloudy — stormy

Activities

ride a bike — fly a kite — make a snowman — go for a walk

go to the beach — read a book — take a photo — watch TV

Social Science

freezing — cold — warm — hot

Picture dictionary

Pearson Education Limited
Edinburgh Gate
Harlow
Essex CM20 2JE
England
and Associated Companies throughout the world.

Poptropica® English Islands

© Pearson Education Limited 2017

Editorial and project management by hyphen

All rights reserved; no part of this publication may be reproduced, stored in a retrieval system, or transmitted in any form or by any means, electronic, mechanical, photocopying, recording, or otherwise without the prior written permission of the Publishers.

First published 2017

ISBN: 978-1-2921-9828-6

Set in Fiendstar 17/21pt

Acknowledgements: The publisher would like to thank Linnette Ansel Erocak, Tessa Lochowski, Laura Miller and José Luis Morales, Steve Elsworth, and Jim Rose for their contributions to this edition.

Illustrators: Chan Sui Fai, Adam Clay, Moreno Chiacchiera (Beehive Illustration), Tom Heard (The Bright Agency), Andrew Hennessey, Marek Jagucki, Sue King (Plum Pudding Illustration), Stephanine Lau, Katie McDee, Bill McGuire (Shannon Associates), Jackie Stafford, Olimpia Wong and Yam Wai Lun

Picture Credits: The publisher would like to thank the following for their kind permission to reproduce their photographs:

(Key: b-bottom; c-centre; l-left; r-right; t-top)

123RF.com: 106 (nod), 108 (hen), 109 (pizza), 109 (rice), Jacek Chabraszewski 106 (wave), Jose Manuel Gelpi Diaz 106 (point), David Franklin 110 (hat), isselee 108 (goat), nrey 108 (duck); **Alamy Stock Photo:** MIXA 106 (stamp feet); **Fotolia.com:** Robert Kneschke 35cr; **Pearson Education Ltd:** Studio 8 104 (car), 106 (move legs), Trevor Clifford 106 (clap), Rafal Trubisz 104 (doll), 106 (shake); **Shutterstock.com:** Ilya Akinshin 104 (kite), AM-STUDiO 104 (teddy bear), Blend Images 35r, Nikolay Dimitrov - ecobo 104 (train), Christopher Elwell 108 (turkey), hamurishi 104 (bike), Eric Isselee 108 (cow), 108 (horse), 108 (sheep), Karkas 110 (jacket), 110 (shoes), 110 (skirt), MShev 106 (touch toes), Maks Narodenko 109 (apples), 109 (bananas), Nattika 109 (eggs), Olga Nayashkova 109 (salad), Nitr 109 (burger), Richard Peterson 104 (ball), Olga Popova 110 (socks), pzAxe 110 (dress), sevenke 110 (T-shirt), Roman Sigaev 110 (trousers), tetxu 109 (fish), Dani Vincek 109 (chicken), Becky Wass 35l, wavebreakmedia 35cl, Mark Yuill 104 (boat)

Cover images: *Back:* **Fotolia.com:** frender r; **Shutterstock.com:** Denys Prykhodov l

All other images © Pearson Education

Every effort has been made to trace the copyright holders and we apologize in advance for any unintentional omissions. We would be pleased to insert the appropriate acknowledgement in any subsequent edition of this publication.